ONE GOD LOGIC'S
LITTLE BOOK OF:
THE

TRUTH

OF

SALVATION

BY: KENNETH J. ESTER

John 8:32 (NASB)

    32 and you will know the truth, and the truth will set you free."

DEDICATION

With all of my heart, this book is dedicated to my Lord and my God, Jesus Christ. For through Him, I know I have salvation and I can only pray that this book will even be a seed that will one day lead others to find that same faith as I have.

CONTENTS

ACKNOWLEDGMENTS

I would like to give a special thanks to everyone who God has used through the years to mold me into who I am today. With a special thanks to the following…

My mother for instilling so many good morals as she raised me, as well as her strength and commitment in her faith to God.

Dawayne and Sheri Morgan for being the best friends anyone could have ever asked for. I hope they someday understand how much I regret that I was not a better friend to them.

My friend Stephen Punturiere for being the only friend I had for many years. Giving me someone to talk to while I struggled through my own personal hell.

Skip Metzger for being that friend who God placed in my life to guide me into a new and awesome relationship with Him.

Ken Cayce for answering so many questions and not losing patience as I studied for God's Truth.

1 - The Question

Do you truly care about following God's' truth?

Your natural response to that might be something in the lines of "Well of course I am!" The problem is that many who say they look to follow God's truth, actually care more about supporting the beliefs they already keep. If someone comes along and shows them how they are wrong, they are not willing to accept it.

Too often we let pride get in the way. Nobody wants to believe they are wrong. Nobody wants to think that the beloved pastor of their church would ever teach them a false doctrine. They don't want to believe their parents and friends would teach them wrong. What they don't understand is that their family and friends can only tell them what they know and if they are taught wrong, they will teach wrong. Their pastor? He is in a different position altogether.

Most pastors belong to specific denominations. They will only teach according to the beliefs of that denomination. Even if they were to find out those beliefs were wrong, they are still bound by guidelines to teach what that denomination tells them is correct. Most churches today are basically corporations and they need to follow the guidelines they are told to follow.

I am not saying that pastors will intentionally deceive you. There are some who will, but most do not. The reason they are in that denomination is because they agree with those beliefs. So they are teaching you what they truly believe to be the truth of God's Word. But that does not mean it *is* the truth of God's Word. The problem lies in the way they are taught to study the Bible.

There is a good chance you have been told at one point in the past that when you read or study God's Word, you should pray first. Ask God to reveal the truth of His words to you. Pray that the Holy Spirit will guide you to the correct interpretations. Likely your pastor believes this same thing. He was taught by the pastors before him to do this as well. This is not necessarily wrong. We should always pray and ask God to guide us in everything we do.

Then we start digging into the Bible with a particular set of beliefs already in place and we look for scriptures to support those beliefs. When we find a verse that we interpret to support the belief we are studying, we take it as confirmation our belief is correct and the Holy Spirit did in fact guide us to the truth. Most every pastor does this. Every pastor of every denomination does it. So let me ask you this. Why are there so many denominations?

Today there are literally thousands of denominations in Christianity. All of them claim that God led them to the correct interpretations of His word. Yet they all teach different variations of Bible doctrines. How is that possible? Logically speaking, if God actually guided them to the truth, we would only have one denomination in the world today. Yet we have thousands.

Yes, we should trust the Holy Spirit to guide us. Yes we should ask God to reveal the truth to us. There are three mistakes almost everyone makes however.

1) We trust our own abilities to always know the difference between our own thoughts and the voice of God.

2) We look for scriptures to support what we already believe.

3) We try to interpret God's Word!

The Voice of God

We want to believe we can hear God speak to us. So many new Christians are taught that God does not speak to us audibly so much. We learn to be quiet and listen to the small voice inside us. With experience, you learn to know God's voice. Did you know that is not even biblical?

In the entire Bible, God never once speaks to someone as a small and still voice inside their minds or hearts. Every single time that God speaks to someone, He does it audibly! There is never a case where God speaks to someone and they do not hear Him the first time either. If God actually speaks to you, you will hear it!

God can and will guide us through urgings and feelings. The problem is even in scripture, they never get everything right. Quite often in Paul's letters, he is warning others to be careful of false teachings and such. So he clearly understood that the Christians of the first century, many who actually witnessed Jesus alive, were not always tuned into the Holy Spirit correctly. If they were, they would always get everything right. Simply put, mankind often does not know the difference between God's voice, his own thoughts, and a cool breeze blowing in his ear. That is why we are told to test every spirit. That includes the Holy Spirit. We don't double check what God tells us because we don't trust God. We should double check God because we cannot trust ourselves to always know God's direction.

Supporting Scriptures

As I have pointed out already, there are thousands of denominations. All of them teach different variations of Bible doctrines. In other words, there are a lot of false doctrines being taught. Yet those false doctrines they teach are not just lies created to be deceiving. They are beliefs based on their interpretations of God's Words.

Every false doctrine is supported by scripture. They are supported by misinterpreting scripture, but they are still supported by scripture.

When someone studies the Bible and they find scripture that supports what they believe, they tend to raise their hands and say "Hallelujah!" and believe that God lead them to that verse as confirmation. Never considering that if their belief is wrong, they might still find verses that can be interpreted to support that false doctrine.

Every false doctrine is supported by scripture. So finding verses that support what you believe is not proof that you have it right. But because people always seem to think it does, they continue to follow false doctrines. Never understanding that they are following false interpretations of God's Word.

How do you keep from falling victim to this? I will get to that later. For now I only want you to recognize that just because scripture can be interpreted to support a belief, doesn't mean that belief is correct.

Interpreting God's Word

I believe one of the greatest lies the devil has every pushed on the people, is that God's Word is this great mystery that needs to be interpreted to understand. That if we want the truth, we need the guidance of the Holy Spirit to interpret it so we can know the truth. This way everyone is trying to interpret God's Word and arguing over what verses mean. This lie had caused many debates and much division in Christianity. It is the crux of why we have so many different denominations.

People fell for that lie. So they began trying to interpret the scriptures and trusting their own ability to know the voice of God and know the guidance of the Holy Spirit. In reality they were trusting their own thoughts and coming up with their own interpretations.

Because the vast majority of Christians are not to be bothered with studying God's Word for themselves, they are nothing more than sheep, being led down a dark road. Never knowing they are being led in the wrong direction.

Basically the Christianity have truly become a cycle of the Blind leading the Blind.

Just imagine how powerful the Christianity community would be if there was no division. If we all followed on set of doctrines and instead of fighting each other, we were all focused on reaching the unsaved. Imagine how much more powerful our message would be if the world saw 2 billion strong all over the world teaching the exact same message!

The truth is, God's Word is not meant to be interpreted. It is actually quite plainly written. Every doctrine has primary scriptures that tell us the truth.

More on Primary scriptures is to come.

I repeat the Question

So I have to ask you again. Do you truly care about following God's' truth? Or are you more worried about supporting what you already believe? If you are faced with a truth of salvation that is not the same as you have already been taught, are you willing to accept that? Or will pride get in the way because you don't want to imagine you were taught wrong?

I hope that what you learn in this book will be what you were already taught. I really do. I hope just as much that if it isn't, that what I show you will in the least pique your interest enough to make you wonder. At best it will set a fire in you to dig in to the Word of God and find the truth for yourself.

I do not want you to be like sheep, being led blindly and believing everything your pastors tell you. I do not want you to believe anything I tell you blindly. I only want you to take what I say and check it all out for yourself. See the truth for yourself.

I hope what I show you in this book will be enough proof to show you the truth. I will be backing everything up with scripture. Not man's interpretation of scripture, but the truth of God. How can I do that? You will see soon enough.

Studying God's Word!

When studying the Bible, I believe it is extremely important to follow some very strict guidelines. These guidelines keep me from falling for false doctrines and they help me find God's truth and not man's interpretations.

1) Context is key. -- Do not just read a verse on its own
and try to interpret it. It is important to always read a
scripture in context. Read the verses around it, even the entire
chapter, and learn what it is talking about. There are too many
scriptures people misinterpret simply because they don't read
what is around it.

2) Do **not cherry pick!** -- All of God's Word must be
considered. Even if you think you have a verse that proves
your point, you need to look at all the scriptures on that
subject and find the whole truth.

3) God is perfect! -- God's Word cannot have any direct
contradictions to theology. If you find a contradiction, there
are three possible causes. There was a copyist mistake, there
was a translation error, or you simply are not interpreting it
correctly. The fault however is always on man and not on
God.

4) God's truth is in the Primary scriptures! -- A primary
scripture is any scripture that is so plainly stated, that there
can only be one logical interpretation. It means exactly what is
says. If a verse states something plainly, then it must be God's
truth. To contradict it is to add a contradiction to God's Word.
So a Primary scripture will always hold higher authority over
any interpreted verse. If there seems to be two Primary
scriptures that contradict each other, the only acceptable
answer is that one of them must have an error in its
translation or have an alternate interpretation you have not
considered.

Primary verses are the key to finding God's truth and not
man's interpretation.

5) Compare Bible Versions. -- A lot of people are taught that the KJV is the only version you can trust. That simply is not true. The KJV is not even the most accurate version out there anymore. Not even close. It was an amazing job of translation for what they had to work with in 1611, but we have literally thousands more ancient manuscripts today and many of them are a lot older than what they had to translate the King James Bible. The verses that were removed in modern versions were removed because they are not in the oldest manuscripts. The modern versions do not have missing scriptures. The KJV has extra scriptures that were not in the original manuscripts.

There is no perfect version of the Bible. They all have some flaws due to copyist errors or translation errors. If you stick to only one version, you constrain yourself to the same flaws that are in that version. The only way you can truly find God's whole truth, is to compare different versions.

If someone follows all of these rules, they can honestly find the truth of God's Word. Not man's interpretation but God's own truth. These rules cannot be ignored, and if you do ignore them, you risk falling victim to false doctrines.

2 - Doctrine of Salvation

There are many doctrines being taught on salvation. Some churches teach that we are saved by faith while others say it is by works. Others might say it is by a combination of faith and works, while others will throw in water baptism. There are many that say someone must repent of their sin to be saved. Some love to push the entire Born Again belief. Sadly, there are churches that teach someone can only be saved if they are a member of their denomination. With so many different teachings on salvation, how is anyone to know the truth? What is God's truth? What does God's Word actually teach us for *how* we are saved?

Obviously, every church believes they are teaching according to what God's Word says. All of them seem to have scripture backing up their beliefs, so how can we know which is right?

The first thing I do is gather all the different scriptures used to support different doctrines, then find the ones that are primary scriptures. So far I have found a total of 18 primary scriptures that clearly tell us *'how'* we are saved. There is one by Peter, two by Luke, six by Paul and nine by Jesus Himself.

<u>Peter (1)</u>

1 Peter 1:8-9 (NASB)
    8 and though you have not seen Him, you love Him, and though you do not see Him now, but believe in Him, you greatly rejoice with joy inexpressible and full of glory,   9 obtaining as the outcome of your faith the salvation of your souls.

<u>Luke (2)</u>

Acts 2:21 (NASB)
    21 'And it shall be that everyone who calls on the name of the Lord will be saved.'

Acts 16:31 (NASB)
    31 They said, "Believe in the Lord Jesus, and you will be saved, you and your household."

<u>Paul (6)</u>

Romans 1:16 (NASB)
    16 For I am not ashamed of the gospel, for it is the power of God for salvation to everyone who believes, to the Jew first and also to the Greek.

Romans 10:9-10 (NASB)
    9 that if you confess with your mouth Jesus as Lord, and believe in your heart that God raised Him from the dead, you will be saved; 10 for with the heart a person believes, resulting in righteousness, and with the mouth he confesses, resulting in salvation.

<u>Paul</u> Continued…

Ephesians 1:13 (NASB)

13 In Him, you also, after listening to the message of truth, the gospel of your salvation—having also believed, you were sealed in Him with the Holy Spirit of promise,

Ephesians 2:8-9 (NASB)

8 For by grace you have been saved through faith; and that not of yourselves, it is the gift of God; 9 not as a result of works, so that no one may boast.

2 Thessalonians 2:13 (NASB)

13 But we should always give thanks to God for you, brethren beloved by the Lord, because God has chosen you from the beginning for salvation through sanctification by the Spirit and faith in the truth.

2 Timothy 3:15 (NASB)

15 and that from childhood you have known the sacred writings which are able to give you the wisdom that leads to salvation through faith which is in Christ Jesus.

<u>Jesus Christ (9)</u>

Luke 7:50 (NASB)

50 And He said to the woman, "Your faith has saved you; go in peace."

John 3:15 (NASB)

15 so that whoever believes will in Him have eternal life.

<u>**Jesus Christ**</u> Continued…

John 3:16 (NASB)

16 "For God so loved the world, that He gave His only begotten Son, that whoever believes in Him shall not perish, but have eternal life.

John 3:18 (NASB)

18 He who believes in Him is not judged; he who does not believe has been judged already, because he has not believed in the name of the only begotten Son of God.

John 5:24 (NASB)

24 "Truly, truly, I say to you, he who hears My word, and believes Him who sent Me, has eternal life, and does not come into judgment, but has passed out of death into life.

John 6:40 (NASB)

40 For this is the will of My Father, that everyone who beholds the Son and believes in Him will have eternal life, and I Myself will raise him up on the last day."

John 6:47 (NASB)

47 Truly, truly, I say to you, he who believes has eternal life.

John 8:24 (NASB)

24 Therefore I said to you that you will die in your sins; for unless you believe that I am He, you will die in your sins."

John 11:25-26 (NASB)

25 Jesus said to her, "I am the resurrection and the life; he who believes in Me will live even if he dies, 26 and everyone who lives and believes in Me will never die. Do you believe this?

All 18 of those scriptures are primary scriptures. They are clearly about salvation. They tell us straight out *how* we are saved. Most importantly however, not a single one of them mentions that we are saved by any means other than believing in Jesus.

Now I am sure some who read this will be thinking of other scriptures that say we are saved by other means. There are several scriptures that are interpreted to mean as much, but the truth is, not one of those are a primary verse. They are all scriptures that are only interpreted to mean something they never actually say, and I will address those scriptures in the coming chapters. For now, what we have here are 18 verses where either Jesus or the writers of the New Testament tell us plainly how we are saved, and every one of them is by faith in Jesus and nothing else.

3 - Saved by Works?

James 2:14-17 (NASB)

14 What use is it, my brethren, if someone says he has faith but he has no works? Can that faith save him? 15 If a brother or sister is without clothing and in need of daily food, 16 and one of you says to them, "Go in peace, be warmed and be filled," and yet you do not give them what is necessary for their body, what use is that? 17 Even so faith, if it has no works, is dead, being by itself.

A common interpretation of this scripture is that it means we are saved by a combination of faith and works. Some churches say it means we are saved by works alone. When I read this scripture, I fail to see where it says either one of those things.

Don't get me wrong. I can definitely see where one can interpret this scripture to mean we are saved by works, but it never actually says it. You need to interpret it to mean something it never says, in order to believe we are saved by works.

When you look at what James actually says, he is telling us that if one has true faith, the kind that is from the heart and actually saves us, it will result in doing good works. Your works is a way to gauge your faith. If your faith does not result in good works, it is dead and does you no good. For if it was true faith, the kind that saves you, you would naturally want to do good things for others.

James is not saying that good works is the cause of salvation. He is saying that good works is the result of true faith.

Now you can argue that is just my interpretation and you interpret it to say we are saved by works. Who is to say which one is right! ... Right? How we interpret what he actually means will depend on what we already believe. But can one believe that the one verse that they have to support their belief is proven by their interpretation of that verse? Doesn't it only make sense that the truth will be the interpretation that fits the rest of God's Word?

How many other scriptures tell us we are actually saved by works? There is not a single verse that ever states that plainly. Yet I have already given 18 scriptures saying we are saved by faith and not one of them mentions works. In fact, I can even give a very clear scripture that says we are *not* saved by works.

Ephesians 2:8-9 (NASB)

8 For by grace you have been saved through faith; and that not of yourselves, it is the gift of God; 9 not as a result of works, so that no one may boast.

There are several points made in this scripture. I would like to look at these points and break it down so we can truly understand what this scripture is saying.

We are saved by God's grace.

We are saved through faith.

Salvation is a gift from God.

It is not of our own doing, and it is not a result of works, so that we will not boast.

1) *For by grace you have been saved* -- If you look up the word 'grace' in the dictionary, it basically means the same thing as 'goodwill'. So this is simply saying that it is by the goodwill of God that we are saved. This is not 'how' we are saved, but it is 'why' God saves us.

2) *through faith;* -- This is the 'how' we are saved. Through faith! When you read other primary scriptures, you know it is through faith in Jesus Christ.

3) *and that not of yourselves, it is the gift of God;* -- This clearly says it is nothing that we do. Salvation is a gift from God. The thing about a gift is that it must be free. If you have to pay for a gift, it is not a gift but it is a purchase. If you have to do anything for it, it is no longer a gift, but it is a reward. To be a gift, it has to be offered for free.

4) *not as a result of works, so that no one may boast.* -- Here we have the scripture clearly saying salvation is not a result of works. Why? Because if we were saved by our own works, people could then boast that they saved themselves. Salvation must be offered as a free gift in order for God to truly say that He saves us and we do not save ourselves.

If you wished, you could put many verses in front of me about how we are commanded to obey the Lord, or follow His commandments. There are several places where Jesus tells us to do good works. I do not deny that, but do you know what you will never find? A single scripture where we are told we must obey God or do good works or we will go to hell.

The common mistake is interpreting scripture that is about having a better relationship with the Lord as a scripture about salvation.

Imagine having children and you live in an area where there are very venomous snakes. You lay down all kinds of rules for them. No getting into the cookie jar without asking first. No sneaking out at night. No fighting with each other. No TV after 9:00 at night. You give them many other rules as well. Then you lay one final rule. Do not go near these snakes. If you do, you will die. Now your children likely will break all of your rules at one time or another. They will upset you when they do. However, if one of them breaks that rule about the snakes, the consequence is more than just upsetting you. It means they will die. Just because you lay down rules about staying alive, does not mean that every rule will cause death if broken.

The Lord wants us to do good works. He commands us to. If we have true faith, we will naturally want to do good things. But those good works do not save us and the Word of God never says they do. Man only has a habit of interpreting scriptures to mean they do.

To believe we are saved by works, you are following man's interpretation over what God's Word actually says.

4 - Saved by Water Baptism?

There are a few verses that can be interpreted to mean we are saved by water baptism. The problem is, in every case, you need to add something to the wording to make it mean we are saved by water baptism. They never actually fully say it.

Matthew 28:19-20 (NASB)

19 Go, therefore, and make disciples of all the nations, baptizing them in the name of the Father and the Son and the Holy Spirit, 20 teaching them to follow all that I commanded you; and behold, I am with you always, to the end of the age."

Clearly this scripture tells us to be baptized right? I fully agree with this. The problem is that nobody is arguing over whether we should be baptized or not. Most all denominations agree that we should all be baptized. What this scripture does not say however, is that it is necessary to be saved. It only says that Jesus commands us to do it. Never that we must do it or we will go to hell.

Mark 16:16 (NASB)

16 He who has believed and has been baptized shall be saved; but he who has disbelieved shall be condemned.

Once again, this verse can easily be interpreted to mean we are saved by water baptism, but it never actually says it. You know what it is missing? The word 'water'!

There are two baptisms in the Bible. Water baptism and baptism of the Spirit. What many Christians do not understand is that the very moment we hear the gospel and we believe, God sends the Holy Spirit to seal us with the promise of salvation. That is baptism of the Spirit, as we learn from this next verse.

Ephesians 1:13 (NASB)

13 In Him, you also, after listening to the message of truth, the gospel of your salvation- having also believed, you were sealed in Him with the Holy Spirit of promise,

Think about what Mark 16:16 actually says. He who believes and is baptized will be saved. He who doesn't believe will not be saved. If this is speaking of water baptism, it leaves a particular group of people out. What about those who believe and are not baptized? Are they saved or not? It doesn't say! The only way this actually makes sense is if it is speaking of baptism of the Spirit and not water baptism. For everyone who truly believes in their heart, is automatically given the Holy Spirit, so they are already baptized in the spirit.

You may be wondering, if it boils down to only those who believe or do not believe, why would He even mention baptism at all? Because it is the way He chose to emphasize the level of belief.

It is possible to believe something with our mind and not in our heart. How often have we heard someone say the president of the United States is "not my president"! They don't accept it in their heart. However if you offered them $50 if they can name the president of the United States, they have no problem naming the president. Because they have accepted the fact in their mind.

So we can believe in Jesus in our mind and not in our heart. To believe with your heart means to be saved. To only believe in your mind means you will not be saved. However, when it comes to not believing, if you don't believe in either your heart or your mind, it makes no difference. You still will not be saved.

It was not important to clarify the difference for the unbeliever because either way they are going to be condemned. But for the believer? It was important to clarify that one needs to believe enough that they receive the baptism of the Holy Spirit to be saved.

Here is yet another scripture that many will interpret to mean we must be baptized by water to be saved.

John 3:5 (NASB)
5 Jesus answered, "Truly, truly, I say to you, unless one is born of water and the spirit, he cannot enter into the kingdom of God.

Now clearly this differentiates baptism of the spirit and water baptism and says both are necessary right? Not necessarily.

Do you notice a very important word that Jesus blatantly leaves out? The word is "baptized". If Jesus was saying we needed to be baptized by water and of the spirit, He would have used that word. He doesn't. He says unless one is "born" of water and spirit.

Now this one is a bit more difficult to explain because I will need to touch on another doctrine that many do not believe. It is called 'predestination'. So I am going to break it all down, bit by bit for you.

The truth is, before we are saved, when we are still in our sinful state, we cannot choose God. We are not even able to do so.

Romans 8:7-8 (NASB)

7 because the mind set on the flesh is hostile toward God; for it does not subject itself to the law of God, for it is not even able to do so, 8 and those who are in the flesh cannot please God.

In order for any sinner to turn to God and accept Jesus as Lord, God must first choose them.

John 6:65 (NASB)

65 And He was saying, "For this reason I have said to you, that no one can come to Me unless it has been granted him from the Father."

Ephesians 1:4 (NASB)

4   just as He chose us in Him before the foundation of the world, that we would be holy and blameless before Him. In love   5   He predestined us to adoption as sons through Jesus Christ to Himself, according to the kind intention of His will,

This is a hard one for many to accept because they cannot help but think it is unfair that God would choose some to save, and not choose others. They believe that it is unfair to those who go to hell because they never had a chance to turn to Christ if God never changed them. That is because they do not understand 'how' God chooses us. He does it through foreknowledge.

1 Peter 1:1-2 (NASB)

1 Peter, an apostle of Jesus Christ,

To those who reside as strangers, scattered throughout Pontus, Galatia, Cappadocia, Asia, and Bithynia, who are chosen2 according to the foreknowledge of God the Father, by the sanctifying work of the Spirit, to obey Jesus Christ and be sprinkled with His blood: May grace and peace be yours in the fullest measure.

You see, God is perfect! He is all knowing! He doesn't only know what we have done and what we will do, but God knows all of the "what if's" as well. What if God was to change someone, would they accept Him or not? What if He changed them today or tomorrow or the day after or any time of their life? God knows who would accept Jesus if He was to change them at any point in their life and those are the ones He chooses to change at just the right moment. If God does not choose someone, it is simply because they were never going to accept Jesus at any point of their life.

Still, some have difficulty accepting this because they feel it's just not fair if God doesn't at least give them a chance. To believe that, they are assuming there is even a tiny chance God could be wrong, and there is not. God is not mostly knowing, He is "All Knowing"! If God says they were not going to accept Jesus as their Lord, there is absolutely no chance they were ever going to. So God chooses not to waste His time changing them.

So what does God do to change us?

Ezekiel 36:25-26 (NASB)

25 Then I will sprinkle clean water on you, and you will be clean; I will cleanse you from all your filthiness and from all your idols. 26 Moreover, I will give you a new heart and put a new spirit within you; and I will remove the heart of stone from your flesh and give you a heart of flesh.

So for someone to accept Jesus as their Lord and Savior, He must first change them so they are able to choose Him. He changes them by sprinkling clean water on them and washes them clean. (That is being born of water.) He gives them a new spirit. (That is being born of spirit.) This all happens the moment someone hears the Gospel and believes with all of their heart. This is being born of water and of Spirit. This brings us in full circle, so that all 18 of the Primary verses about being saved by believing in Jesus and by no other means are still 100% correct.

There is yet one more scripture that is often used to say we must be baptized by water to be saved.

1 Peter 3:21 (NASB)

21 Corresponding to that, baptism now saves you—not the removal of dirt from the flesh, but an appeal to God for a good conscience—through the resurrection of Jesus Christ,

How one interprets this verse can be due to which version of the Bible they use. It is why I believe that if you are going to study the Word of God (not just read it), it is best to use versions that are more accurate word for word as well as compare versions. This is one of the cases where I do not believe the KJV Bible is the best to use.

Some versions will translate it so it seems as if we are now saved by water baptism. However that is not what it is actually telling us here.

Let's take a look at the Berean Study Bible for instance…

21 And this water symbolizes the baptism that now saves you also—not the removal of dirt from the body, but the pledge of a clear conscience toward God—through the resurrection of Jesus Christ,

This is the closest word for word. The key word here is "symbolizes". It is translated from the Greek word "antitypon".

We are not being told that water baptism saves us. We are only being told that the water symbolizes the baptism that saves us. The burial and resurrection of the Lord Jesus Christ.

Every scripture that is used to support that we must be baptized by water to be saved, is nothing more than a man's interpretation to mean something the verse never actually says. There is not one primary verse telling us we are saved by water baptism. As I have mentioned a few times already, there are 18 primary scriptures saying we are saved by believing in Jesus and not one of those mentions water baptism. So again, will you believe the interpretations of man, or will you accept the truth of what God's Word actually says?

5– Saved by Repenting of Sin?

There are many scriptures one can give, telling us to repent. The problem with all of these scriptures is simply that they do not understand the correct definition of the word "repent". Many preachers today will teach that it means to turn away from sin. This is a false teaching.

The Greek word 'metanoia' is translated to 'repent'. Its definition is to have a change of mind, or a change of heart. I have heard some say its meaning goes deeper in the sense that it is a spiritual change. The simple fact is however, it has nothing to do with sin unless the verse literally says to repent of sin.

Every scripture that says to repent and be saved, never mentions anything about sin. So these verses only mean to have a change of heart and be saved. Which is exactly what happens when one hears the gospel and believes with all their heart that Jesus is Lord. The moment they believed, they had a change of heart. They repented!

Every time a scripture mentions repenting from sin, it never mentions salvation. They are telling us to turn away from sin, but there is no reason to believe it means to turn away from sin or you will go to hell.

6 - Does Sin Send Us to Hell?

If God's Word does not actually tell us that need to repent from sin to be saved, and it says we only need to truly believe in Jesus, does that mean the sins we commit will not send us to hell? The quick answer to that is yes! The truth is, the sins we commit do not send us to hell!

And again, this is likely a place where some of you are huffing and puffing, want to throw scriptures at me that say sin sends us to hell. I will get to those.

John 3:18 (NASB)

18 The one who believes in Him is not judged; the one who does not believe has been judged already, because he has not believed in the name of the only Son of God.

Think about what this verse says. If someone believes in Jesus, they will not be judged. If they do not believe, they are already judged. Not because they haven't repented of sin, but simply because they did not believe. Sin is left out of this altogether!

If the sins we commit could send us to hell, that would mean this verse is wrong. It would mean this verse should be saying those who believe and repent from sin will not be judged and those who do not repent from sin are already judged. But it never mentions sin or repenting from sin. It only mentions believing!

Jesus says if you believe, you go to heaven. In fact, He says that very clearly 9 times in the Bible. Never mentioning any clauses like, "If you ask forgiveness of your sins". Then He takes it a step further by saying that if one does not believe, they are going to hell.

The truth is, there is not one verse in the Bible that says the sins we commit will send us to hell? Some might want to throw this at me...

1 Corinthians 6:9-10 (NASB)

9 Or do you not know that the unrighteous will not inherit the kingdom of God? Do not be deceived; neither the sexually immoral, nor idolaters, nor adulterers, nor homosexuals, 10 nor thieves, nor the greedy, nor those habitually drunk, nor verbal abusers, nor swindlers, will inherit the kingdom of God.

To really understand what this scripture is teaching, you need to understand a few things first.

1) Paul is writing to other believers. Not unbelievers here.

2) The Bible thinks of the word "sinner" as a title. Not a noun. Christians like to say that if someone runs, they are a runner, so if they sin, they are a sinner. That is only true if you use it as a noun. The Bible sees the sinner as the unbeliever and I will even prove that out with this very scripture.

3) Everyone sins. Not just the unbeliever, but everyone.

1 John 1:8 (NASB)

8 If we say that we have no sin, we are deceiving ourselves, and the truth is not in us.

John clearly uses words like "we", "ourselves" and "us". He is including himself in this statement. He is admitting that he, an apostle, still sins.

And Paul says this...

Romans 3:23 (NASB)

23 for all have sinned and fall short of the glory of God,

So if John and Paul, both apostles, say we all sin and include themselves. It's fairly safe to say that everyone sins. Yet, 1 Corinthians 6:9-10 clearly says if we sin we will go to hell right? Not at all. All you have to do is read the very next verse, which everyone so conveniently seems to skip past.

1 Corinthians 6:11 (NASB)

11 Such were some of you; but you were washed, but you were sanctified, but you were justified in the name of the Lord Jesus Christ and in the Spirit of our God.

Paul was not telling us that anyone who commits a sin will go to hell. In fact in verses 9 and 10, Paul was not even listing different sins. He was listing different types of sinners. An Idolater is a sinner. Idolatry would be the sin. All of these mentioned are types of sinners.

Then in verse 11, Paul says "Such were some of you". He didn't say they still are, but they "were" these sinners. Yet as I have shown, Paul and John both say we all still sin. If you believe that sin sends us to hell, then you have a clear contradiction you need to deal with here. How can they say everyone sins, then Paul turn around and write to the church and say they are no longer sinners? The only way to clarify this without there being a contradiction in God's Word, is to recognize that a sinner is an unbeliever.

Paul was telling them that they used to be these sinners, but they are no longer because they have been washed clean, sanctified and justified in the name of Jesus Christ.

Though we still sin and fall short, we are washed clean and still going to heaven.

So, if 1 Corinthians 6:9-10 is not a verse to prove that our sins will send us to hell, what is then?

Go back and read through all of the primary verse I listed on how we are saved. If sin could send us to hell, how would that work with those verses?

We are saved by believing with all our hearts that Jesus is the Son of God, that He died on the cross and rose from the dead and His sacrifice saves us. We are saved by believing with all our hearts that Jesus is Lord. Believing it enough that we are willing to say it out loud where others can hear.

The truth is, the sins we commit do not send us to hell. I know this can be a tough thing for many to accept, as it is so completely the opposite of what most churches teach. But they teach that because they interpret scripture to mean what it never says. That and to be honest, because they do not completely understand how salvation works. They know specifics but they struggle to explain it in a way that someone can truly understand it.

The consequences of sin are not hell, as many churches teach. The consequences of sin are two fold.

1) Because God gives us a new spirit, our spirit can no longer be happy in sin. It finds its happiness in being closer to God. When a believer falls into sin, they are never happy. They are miserable. No true believer is going to be happy in

sin. The further away from God you fall, the more miserably they get.

2) Sin eats away our rewards in the afterlife. Churches often teach about going to heaven, but that is only temporary. The truth is after the day of judgment, this earth will pass away and God will give to us a new earth. It is on that earth where we will live new lives in our glorified bodies. There will be different levels of authority and jobs and everything just like in this life. Those who earned greater rewards will get greater positions. Those who eat away their rewards with sin, will be servants and laborers. These lives last forever with no chance of ever moving up. If you think about it that is a heavy consequence to sin.

When I teach that sin will not send us to hell, a lot of people think I am saying a Christian gets the best of both worlds. We can live in sin and still go to heaven. Though that is technically true that we can live in sin and still go to heaven, it is far from the best of both worlds. It is literally the worst of both worlds. Living in sin makes us miserable in this world and gives us fewer rewards in the next.

7 - Understanding Salvation

If we are going to be honest, we can look at scriptures all day long about how we are saved through believing in Jesus as our Lord and Savior, but we still won't really understand it. Proving doctrines to be true or false according to scripture doesn't help anyone make sense of it all. Yes Jesus died on the cross, but why did He have to die on the cross? Why did He even need to die? Couldn't God have just decided to forgive us for our sins without needing to go through all the suffering? How does one put all the information together and make sense of it all? To help you truly understand salvation, it helps to first understand a few other things.

Jesus is God

Not only is Jesus the only begotten Son of God, but Jesus is also God in the flesh.

In Revelation 19, Jesus is preparing to return in the Second Coming when He will battle in Armageddon. We learn another name for Jesus.

Revelation 19:13 (NASB)

13 He is clothed with a robe dipped in blood, and His name is called The Word of God.

Jesus is the Word of God. We find the Word is mentioned in the Gospel of John as well.

John 1:1 (NASB)
1 In the beginning was the Word, and the Word was with God, and the Word was God.

So here it says the Word, who we already know is Jesus, was God. There are other places where Jesus refers to Himself as God and others call Him the Mighty God and He never corrects them. So it is clear that according to the Bible, Jesus is God in the flesh.

God Forgave Sins in the Old Testament

Most churches teach that Jesus died on the cross so we could be forgiven for our sins. I believed this myself until recently. It is true but not completely correct.

All one has to do is a quick search in the Bible for the word "atonement". You will find many verses where God demands animal sacrifices as an act of atonement. Here are a few of them.

Exodus 29:36 (NASB)
Each day you shall offer a bull as a sin offering for atonement, and you shall purify the altar when you make atonement for it, and you shall anoint it to consecrate it.

Exodus 32:30 (NASB)

And on the next day Moses said to the people, "You yourselves have committed a great sin; and now I am going up to the Lord; perhaps I can make atonement for your sin."

Leviticus 4:31 (NASB)
Then he shall remove all its fat, just as the fat was removed from the sacrifice of peace offerings; and the priest shall offer it up in smoke on the altar as a soothing aroma to the Lord. So the priest shall make atonement for him, and he will be forgiven.

To be clear, atonement is not the same as forgiveness. Atonement is an action one takes to right a wrong in hopes of forgiveness. But why would God demand atonement for sins if He was not willing to forgive those sins? And as you see in Leviticus 4:31, that God plainly says that he will be forgiven. So now there is no debate that God was willing to forgive sins in the Old Testament times. This is very important in order to truly understand salvation.

Importance of Free Will

Most people do not realize it, but the greatest gift God ever gave us, was not salvation. That would be the second greatest gift. The greatest gift was Free Will.

God could have created us perfect, so Adam and Eve nor anyone who was ever born would sin. With no sin, there would be no death. Not sickness. No crime. The world would have been perfect. The problem is that for God to make us so we never sinned, He would have had to make us without free will.

Without free will, we would have no ability to do anything of our own choice. No matter how inconsequential it may seem, if we do it intentionally, we would not be able to do it.

We would sleep because our bodies would naturally fall asleep after so long. We would naturally wake up when our bodies had enough rest, but when we woke up, we would lay there doing nothing. Just staring in whatever direction we were looking when we woke up. We would not even be able to roll our eyes to one side or the other to look at something else unless there was movement to draw our eyes reflexively.

We would just lay there until God told us to get up. We would get up and stare straight ahead like robots and do nothing until God told us what to do. If He told us to get dressed, we wouldn't be able to choose what clothes to put on unless God told us *what* to put on. We could not choose what foods we wanted to eat, what flavor ice-cream to have, what TV shows we wanted to watch or anything. Every tiny little decision we make would be impossible to do on our own. We would essentially be like Ken and Barbie dolls in the hands of a child. We would able to think, but we could not use our thoughts for anything.

God didn't want Ken and Barbie dolls. God created us and He loves what He creates. He loves us enough that He wanted us to actually live life. He wanted us to be able to enjoy life to its fullest. God wanted us to enjoy different flavors and have favorite colors. He wanted us to fall in love and laugh and have amazing lives. He knew before He created Adam and Eve that if He gave them free will, that would also give them the ability to sin and He knew they would sin. He knew they would fall from His grace and it would cause all of the sadness, suffering and hate in this world. He knew before He created them, all of the problems that would come with it. But He loved us enough to put up with it anyway. So He gave them free will. In a strange way, the reason there is so much suffering in this world today, is because God loves us. He loves us enough to allow all of that to happen in order to give us the ability to live life to its fullest.

The Story of Salvation

When God created Adam, He wanted us to live life to its fullest, so he gave him Free Will. He knew well in advance that Adam and Eve would sin and that would cause a lot of suffering in the world for thousands of years. Still, God loved us enough to give us free will anyway. And Adam and Eve sinned.

When they sinned, it did more than just upset God. It stained their soul with sin and because of that, every person ever born was born with a soul corrupted by sin.

Psalm 51:5 (NASB)

5 Behold, I was brought forth in guilt, And in sin my mother conceived me.

Psalm 58:3 (NASB)

3 The wicked have turned away from the womb; These who speak lies go astray from birth.

Ephesians 2:3 (NASB)

3 Among them we too all previously lived in the lusts of our flesh, indulging the desires of the flesh and of the mind, and were by nature children of wrath, just as the rest.

Mankind was essentially separated from God because God was so pure and holy, if He allowed us into heaven, it would literally destroy our souls, for sin cannot exist in His presence.

We know this because when Moses was on the mountain and asked God to show him His glory, this was part of God's reply...

Exodus 33:20 (NASB)
20 He further said, "You cannot see My face, for mankind shall not see Me and live!"

Through time, God was willing to forgive our sins, but there had to be an atonement for our sins. So God allowed mankind to sacrifice animals, offering a blood sacrifice for atonement for their sins. With this, God could forgive the sins they committed and they could continue growing in their relationship with Him.

Unfortunately there was no animal in the world that would ever be pure and holy enough to wash the stain of sin from our souls. So even though God would forgive people for their sins, they still were bound for hell because their souls could never be in His presence in His full glory. It would destroy them.

God had a plan however. When the time was right, He sent the Word to take on flesh and become human. Though the Word was God, He was willing to set His godly powers aside and become a little lower than angels for a little while.

Hebrews 2:9 (NASB)
9 But we do see Him who was made for a little while lower than the angels, namely, Jesus, because of His suffering death crowned with glory and honor, so that by the grace of God He might taste death for everyone.

He was born of a virgin birth, God being His only real Father, and He was given the name Jesus.

Matthew 1:25 (NASB)

25 but kept her a virgin until she gave birth to a Son; and he named Him Jesus.

Now Jesus grew up and gathered His disciples and taught them how God wanted them to live, but that was not His purpose. His mission was to die for us. And die for us He did.

Jesus knew well in advance that He would die for us and even knew *how* He would die. He knew very well what crucifixion entailed. He knew everything they were going to do to Him, and it scared Him. It scared Him so much, that the night they were going to take Him, He went to the garden and prayed, asking the Father to remove Him from having to go through with it.

He prayed so hard that His sweat came out as drops of blood. Today we know this as a rare medical condition called Hematidrosis. Yet as scared as He was, He ended that prayer with "Father let not my will be done, but your will be done." And it was God's will that He go through with it.

Luke 22:42-44 (NASB)

42 saying, "Father, if You are willing, remove this cup from Me; yet not My will, but Yours be done." 43 [Now an angel from heaven appeared to Him, strengthening Him. 44 And being in agony, He was praying very fervently; and His sweat became like drops of blood, falling down upon the ground].

They took Jesus and beat Him. They did not whip Him but they scourged Him. A scourge is a whip with multiple straps of leather with pieces of glass and bone tied along them. When the cords slashed Him, the debris tied into them would dig in and shred through His flesh. The blood loss from the scourging alone would have been terrible. They mocked Him and shoved a crown of thorns into His scalp, then they made Him drag His own cross up the Hill. When they reached the top, they used three spikes to nail His hands and feet to the cross. Then they raised Him up so everyone could watch Him die.

Even as He hung on the cross, suffering immense pain, they continued to ridicule Him. The soldiers gambled for His cloak. Do you know what Jesus did? He asked the Father to forgive them.

Luke 23:34 (NASB)

34 [But Jesus was saying, "Father, forgive them; for they do not know what they are doing."] And they cast lots, dividing His garments among themselves.

There can be no greater forgiveness than to go through what Jesus went through, even though He was never convicted of a single crime, and to still ask the Father to forgive those who had done it to them.

It wasn't just an ordinary man who died on that cross though. Jesus was God in the flesh. A sacrifice so pure and holy that it covers all of our sins and washes the stain of sin from our souls. It cleanses our souls and makes us righteous before God.

Today, God offers salvation to us as a gift. Completely free. We do not have to purchase it. We do not need to do anything to earn it. It is not a reward. It is a gift.

However, the cleansing of our soul is not a physical gift, it is a spiritual gift. And a gift is never yours until you accept it. Ask yourself, how can anyone possibly accept a spiritual gift if they don't believe it is even real?

This is why we must believe with all our hearts that Jesus is the Son of God, that He died on the cross and rose from the dead. We must believe it enough that we are willing to testify of it with our own words. For anyone who truly believes with all their heart will receive the gift of salvation and have their souls cleansed. To truly believe with all your heart, is to receive the gift of salvation. To be an unbeliever is to reject the gift.

We ask God to forgive us for our sins so we can continue to grow closer to Him in our relationship with Him. The cleansing of our soul is what saves us and allows us to enter heaven.

What greater God can there be than one who will become human, suffer immense torture and die to save His creation. Just because He loves us enough to give us Free Will, so we can have the experience of living life to its fullest! How deserving of hell we are if we reject Him after doing that for us?

8 - A Final Message

I have mentioned that the greatest gift God ever gave us was Free Will. That He gave that to us, knowing full well all the problems and misery it would cause in this world. That he gave it to us anyway because He loved us so much and wanted us to be able to experience life to its fullest. I do not doubt that there would be some who read that and think, "Not this life!"

Believe me, I know where you are coming from. My life has not been one filled with joy and happiness. I have had far more go wrong and so very little go right for me. I truly do not like my life. Yet I have had a much better life than many others. There are people who have had terrible lives. Filled with horrible things. You may be wondering how they are supposed to experience life to its fullest.

The truth is, it is not this life that God gave us free will to enjoy. This life is nothing more than the testing ground. A test to separate those who would love the Lord from those who would reject Him. A testing ground for those who reject Him to decide what level their suffering will be, and those who accept Him to find what their rewards will be. The real life He wants us to truly enjoy is the one coming after this one.

The Bible tells us that there is coming a day when He will bring the souls of all the dead believers back with Him and their bodies will be raised as imperishable glorified bodies. As they are reunited with their bodies, those who are still alive will be changed from perishable to imperishable. We will have bodies that no longer age or get sick. We will not suffer injury or die… ever again. We will not be spirit, but we will have glorified bodies and He will destroy this earth and give to us a new earth. A much larger earth, where we will live new lives. Lives where there will be no hatred or suffering. No shame or pain. Lives where we will all be happy. Those who lived their lives for the Lord and did many good deeds will be given much greater rewards. Those who do not will receive fewer rewards. Some will be leaders and have great jobs. Others will be servants and laborers, but everyone will be satisfied with their position and be happy.

That is the life God gave us free will to experience. That is the life we will receive when we accept the gift of salvation. That is the life we will live forever! That life will be far greater than being cast into the Lake of Fire for all eternity.

Books by: Kenneth J. Ester

Bible Doctrine: The Unbiased Truth

One God Logic's Little Books:

Is God Real?
†
The End Times and Salvation
†
The Unbiased truth of the Rapture
†
Jesus Died for the Homosexual Too
†

Feel free to visit my site: **www.OneGodLogic.com**

ABOUT THE AUTHOR

Born in 1966, Kenneth J. Ester was "Born Again" in 1982 and allowed the devil to pull him away. At the end of 2017, God took Him back and put him on a mission to learn and then to teach the truth.

God quickly showed him that he could not trust what the church has taught him in the past and he needed to study His Word and find the Unbiased Truth.

"The Truth is everything to me." He says. "The truth is, I don't know how much time I have left, but I plan on using it to make up for the lifetime of shame I left behind. There is a whole lot of bad teachings out there and I want to teach people the truth. Not my truth or some church's truth, but God's Truth!"